WORK MATTERS

AFTER
DINNER
SPEECHES

WORK MATTERS

AFTER DINNER SPEECHES

—

MARTIN NICHOLLS

WARD LOCK

Dedicated to my grandson Lee, the only member of
the family who, so far, hasn't had to listen to me
making a speech.

© Text Ward Lock Ltd 1989

First published in Great Britain in 1989
by Ward Lock Limited, 8 Clifford Street
London W1X 1RB , a Cassell Company

Text filmset in Times by Columns
Printed and bound in Great Britain by
William Collins and Sons & Co Ltd, Glasgow

British Library Cataloguing in Publication Data

Nicholls, Martin
    After dinner speeches.
    1. Public speaking
    I. Title
    808.5'1

    ISBN 0-7063-6816-9

Contents

Don't deliberately look a freak
Don't arrive late
Do check on arrival
Do make sure your notes are well placed
Do start slowly
Don't distract your audience
Do use the microphone as a friend
Do stand still
Don't fidget
Don't shuffle notes and papers
Do try to be sincere
Do try and use good English
Don't underestimate the intelligence of
 your audience
Do use your notes if you need them
Do keep cool
Don't panic
Do remember to look at your audience
Don't get over-confident
Do watch the time
Do remember your finale

Introduction

Giving a speech can be a very rewarding experience.

You have the satisfaction of knowing you have prepared yourself properly and honed your thoughts and research into a succinct and entertaining speech. Delivered well, such a speech may well lead to the compliment of further invitations to speak at other gatherings.

Why then does the thought of having to stand up and make a speech in public strike a haunting fear in the hearts of most people? A fear that causes sinking feelings in the strongest, the most forceful, and the most fluent of individuals. It affects people who quite happily walk into a room filled with strangers and within minutes are happily chatting to their nearest companions in the most animated way. Why then this fear of the public platform?

After dinner speaking is only a form of communication when reduced to its basic level and if the following can help you to believe in its simplicity, then hopefully a lot of those latent fears can be allayed. However, like any other form of successful communication there are basic rules to follow and pitfalls to avoid.

ENJOY YOURSELF

After dinner speaking should be enjoyed as much by the speaker as the listener.

The intention of this book is to help those less used to after dinner speaking avoid those pitfalls and to learn the basic rules. They do not need to fear being asked to speak but, rather to accept it as an exhilarating challenge. It could turn out to be a most enjoyable experience. It presents an opportunity to express yourself in a new dimension and in new environments and to have fun at the same time.

There is still a very real demand for good, competent, after dinner speakers. The ability to handle yourself, your hosts, your microphones and other technical impedimenta and above all your audience and afterwards to leave for home with a full and happy heart can leave one with an enormous sense of great personal pride and satisfaction.

There is no harm in feeding the ego occasionally, you all have one! My aim in the following pages is to set out the rules and strategies that can ease the pain and fear, and allow you to enjoy that feeling of satisfaction that comes from a job well done.

Although I frequently refer to the person I am talking about as 'he' this is only for the purpose of the smoother flow of the language than saying 'he or she' each time. The comments apply equally to both sexes.

1. Making it a good speech

When you sit back after a good dinner and listen to others speak, you tend to make very simple judgements of their performance:

Do you like them?

Can you hear them?

Have they interested or amused you?

Was it well presented?

Were they relevant?

Were they succinct?

When you prepare a speech if you try and see yourself as your audience will see you, then hopefully you can please them. If you decide to ignore any thought of your audience and set out to prepare a speech that is pure self-indulgence then you must be prepared for the consumer not appreciating the finished article.

If you consider for a moment how your listeners will hear, see and judge you then you are well on the way to avoiding the more obvious mistakes and achieving your goal. The goal challenges, but often eludes, speakers – an audience that is with them all the way.

BE LIKEABLE

The first of your criteria was whether you liked the speaker, or not. In asking this question what you are really saying is 'Is the person standing up there addressing us, someone with whom I can readily identify?' You do not have to share all the views and beliefs expressed. If the speaker is sincere and appears to be talking 'to' you and not 'at' or 'over' you, then there is every chance that you will like and respect him or her.

Cast your mind back to your school days. Wasn't it so much easier to learn from the teacher you liked because he or she was interesting and talked to you more as an equal, than from those who may well have been very clever but never seemed to be on your level or actually communicating with you personally?

A good speaker has to be conscious of this factor when speaking and concentrate on creating an empathy with the audience. His or her aim is to get them to feel that the speech is to each of them individually. Otherwise it can become just an address they happen to be hearing and as a result may or may not concentrate on, as the feeling takes them.

This book aims to help you create that empathy.

BE INTERESTING

A good speech is interesting, it is not, and never should be, a lecture. It is an integral part of the evening as a whole. Proceedings usually begin with a sociable pre-dinner reception, followed by a pleasant meal eaten in enjoyable and congenial company and concluding with the entertainment of the after dinner speeches.

If the evening is considered to be formal in its content, it may well be expected that all or some of the speeches should contain a message or more serious point.

Being interesting starts with choosing your subject matter and approaching it with care. If you can include original ideas or a new slant on a subject, so much the better.

It is also important to be accurate. This not only includes getting your facts right but also making sure you pronounce people's names correctly.

If you build up a well-argued case and have obviously done some careful research you will be well on the way to interesting your audience.

It is easier to transmit the message referred to earlier to an audience which is listening, rather than to one that has been lulled into a stupor by a dull soporific presentation.

To be serious it is not necessary to be boring. One of the most entertaining and amusing speeches I ever heard was given by a very prominent politician of the time, explaining what the balance of payments meant to us all.

PRESENT IT WELL

A well constructed and delivered speech will retain an audience's attention. A rambling, poorly prepared and disorganized speech will soon have the minds of your listeners turning to other things.

The use of very long sentences, for example, without any pauses can prove very difficult for your listeners to absorb. Then there is the added danger that you too may begin to lose the thread of your own thoughts. Short and punchy sentences are easier to deliver and are so much easier for your audience to understand. In helping yourself, you are also helping them. To retain the interest of your audience, remember that each sentence and point you are trying to make, should lead logically into the next one. If you jump from point to point in a totally unco-ordinated manner, your listeners' minds will soon give up the struggle of trying to keep up with you!

Your speech can only ever be of any value to the proceedings and interest to the audience if they can understand it, and retain at least some of it in their minds.

BE AUDIBLE

However good the speech it is no good unless it can be heard. This is perhaps the most obvious of our criteria in judging our speaker. Obvious, yet too frequently it happens that the audience can't and it leaves the speaker in a hopeless position.

There are a variety of reasons for this inaudibility. The basic technical reasons are poor acoustics or failure of the microphones. In the case of technical failure there is no reason why certain obvious steps cannot be taken to improve the situation.

I was once toastmastering a dinner for around a thousand ladies in Brussels when all the microphones failed. At the end of dinner we took the obvious step of inviting the audience to leave their tables and move closer to the top table. The speakers then came down into the audience to address them – not perfect, but at least the vast majority could hear.

To sit at the back of a function, some considerable distance from the speakers, and not to be able to hear a single word is a sure way to destroy anyone's enjoyment.

If you cannot hear a speaker then all is lost. The speaker has every right to expect the organizers to have made sure that he will be heard but the final check is up to him or her. Every speaker should allow time beforehand to undertake a sound check.

Sadly, inaudibility is all too often the fault of the

speaker. Lack of microphone experience coupled with inadequate preparation can lead to the reading of an entire speech in a dull monotone. The speaker's head remains dropped below the level of the microphone's area of sensitivity and this can mean that most of the audience cannot hear.

Speakers who for large parts of their speeches directs their words sideways to those sitting alongside them on the top table soon lose the attention of the rest of the audience.

As a Toastmaster I have been privileged to hear many great speeches and many great speakers. I have on occasions been saddened when listening to good speeches, from my position close to a speaker, to realize that many of the audience were unable to hear clearly. As a result they were talking and distracting those who could hear. In almost every case this was the fault of the speaker and there was no way I could come to his aid once he had started. How I would have loved the opportunity to help.

The ability of your audience to concentrate on your offering is governed by their being able to hear you without having to strain. I hope that later in this book we can ensure that above all else you will be heard.

BE AMUSING

Ideally a good speech is both interesting and amusing.

When you consider whether a speaker has interested or amused you, it is little different from asking whether you actually remember anything from the speech.

To amuse an audience does not necessarily mean

reeling off a string of jokes. Indeed this is not normally the basic requirement of a speaker.

To be funny is much harder than most people imagine. My own view is that the average speaker would be well advised to avoid telling jokes unless he or she is naturally funny or has gained quite a bit of experience. There is no doubt that sincerity in a speaker is far more important than ability as a comedian or comedienne. Having said that however, there is a real place for humour, as opposed to comedy, in a speech.

Everyone of us has a sense of humour, even though, of course, it varies widely from person to person. Our sense of humour is so often our safety valve in times of adversity. It is a part of our everyday existence and our lives are generally richer for it. However, as an important integral part of a speech it probably needs more care and attention than any of the other components.

There is no greater satisfaction than standing in front of an audience which is laughing as a result of your humour. There is no worse sinking feeling than a stony deadpan reaction to what you thought was your most humorous line! Only use homour if you are confident and happy about it. If you have doubts and uncertainties don't try it.

BE RELEVANT

This is an aspect you can control for it is largely a matter of preparation.

Without the right approach it can be surprisingly hard to retain relevance in a speech. Failure to do so usually indicates a lack of preparation. Occasionally it can be the result of the speaker having second thoughts once he is on his feet and becoming side-tracked from his prepared theme.

Danger can arise when a speaker, having done all the right homework and preparation, arrives on the night with considerable nervous doubts. Having spoken for a few moments and overcome that initial nervousness, he or she decides that it is not so difficult after all and starts to depart from their prepared presentation.

To be able to think on your feet is a very useful and necessary attribute, but it should only be used where there is no alternative. The pitfall awaiting the unwary is that it is so easy to digress and lose the continuity, the relevance, that is so important. However interesting your sudden thoughts may be, they do need to be relevant to the basic theme of your address.

BE SUCCINCT

Finally you questioned the ability of the speaker to be succinct. It can be the hardest discipline for a speaker to achieve. To anyone asked to speak at a few moments' notice, five minutes can seem an eternity. Give that same person three months' notice to make a ten-minute speech and they will probably then have the utmost difficulty in condensing their material to match the brief.

It is in many ways better to condense the speech into a shorter time than that requested and retain the audience's interest than to pad it out for the sake of it and lose them as a result.

You may also be doing a discourtesy to your hosts by over-running your allotted period and possibly disrupting the evening's arrangements.

A problem frequently created by function organizers is caused by their belief that a large number of speakers is necessary for a successful evening. It only needs one speaker to stray from his or her time allocation for those who follow to be in difficulties. In the first place, unless the culprit has spoken particularly well, the audience will have begun to lose interest which will be difficult to recapture. Secondly, there may be pressure on those who have still to speak to make up for lost time! The danger then arises of either trying to cut parts of the prepared speech or worse still, attempting to speak somewhat quicker.

Remember you are almost certainly part of an overall plan for the evening and the greatest service you can do your hosts is to honour their instructions as exactly as possible.

PREPARATION IS ALL-IMPORTANT

There can be no substitute for thorough preparation but it is something entirely within your own control.

To most of us after dinner speaking is only an occasional exercise. Most of us will want, however, to perform to the very best of our ability, if only for our own personal pride. Few would consider decorating a room at home without spending more time on the preparation than the decoration. Most of us can, given the time, construct a presentable and well ordered speech. It just needs careful and well ordered preparation, based on simple guidelines.

Your initial thoughts The period of preparation is more mental than physical. It doesn't mean you need to try and write a speech straight off. Once you have been asked to speak at a certain dinner, at a certain place, on a certain date you are immediately aware of the time available to you for preparation. Having been given or chosen the subject there are many odd moments you can spare for thought, moments in which you can begin to collect ideas and sketch a mental pattern for your speech.

This is all before you even consider committing anything to your first written draft. Journeys on trains or buses or cars, time in the bath or in bed are ideal. You can let your thoughts wander to inspire a plan or an idea for that vital content. It was the late great Sir Winston Churchill who used to wander in his garden rehearsing his 'impromptus'.

Make notes It is a good plan to keep a notebook and pen handy so that you can jot down ideas which suddenly occur to you. This way you won't lose a useful phrase or forget a small but important point. You may not use them all but they will be ready if you want them. What is more, you will be surprised how much material you have assembled without apparent effort.

The first draft Set yourself a preliminary deadline a reasonable time before the all-important date to begin writing.

Having gathered your thoughts together over a period you can start drafting your speech. Initially you should prepare a skeleton, the bones of which you can gradually flesh out as you become more positively ordered in your ideas.

As you start to write remember that there is a subtle but positive difference between the written and the spoken word. This can be a positive trap if you try to read your speech word for word when the time comes to deliver it.

You do need to allow time in your preparation to condense your final written draft to lead-phrases or headings in order to ensure that your presentation retains its conversational appeal and does not sound a tedious reading. I shall deal with the discipline of preparation at length later but even at this early stage it must become obvious that there can be no effective short-cut or substitute for a full and considered preparation.

DELIVERY

When the great day dawns it is one thing to have written and prepared a good speech – to deliver it effectively is quite a different discipline.

You need to give as much time and thought to your delivery and presentation as you did to the actual speech preparation. When it comes to standing and addressing your audience it is possible that you may have to make certain adjustments to the way in which you normally speak. You should certainly not consider putting on an unnatural voice to speak – nearly every voice and accent has its own pleasing qualities – but you may need to speak more slowly or in a more pronounced manner than when speaking normally.

You must be prepared to avoid the problems, so often caused by nervousness, that can effect your speaking voice. The most usual effects are the strangulation of the voice, the swallowing of words, the dropping of your voice at the end of sentences and the most common fault, speaking much faster than normal.

You should stand up in the firm belief that your audience want to hear every word you are going to say. Make sure that they do.

CONTROLLING YOUR NERVES

You need to create an ability to appear and behave with an external and natural calm, regardless of how fast your heart may be beating. Hopefully a large measure of this quiet confidence will come from knowing that your speech is as well prepared as you could wish. The remainder should come from the satisfaction of your personal preparation.

You will need to rise to your feet feeling comfortable, safe in the knowledge that you look right for the particular evening and have considered all the various pitfalls. You have made certain that the microphone works. It is in the right position and at the right height for you and you can be heard and seen in all parts of the room.

You have a lectern or other suitable place to hold your notes. You have taken a deep breath and you are ready to face your audience. You have prepared and disciplined yourself to start slowly and calmly and gradually build up your speech as it progresses. You have learnt enough of its content not to have to read it all, and as a result left yourself sufficient flexibility to avoid repeating remarks made by previous speakers without destroying your confidence or content.

THE EVENING ITSELF

To achieve these levels of presentation you need to arrive at your dinner with a totally clear and concentrated mind. That clarity of mind is essential to allow you to think your way into your speech as the evening progresses.

That thinking process on the night will allow you to pick up on remarks and comments of previous speakers and refer to them as you make your own speech. This ability can only be achieved by a calm assurance in your own preparation. It has the added advantage of immediately making your hosts and your audience warm to you, realizing that you have not only come to deliver your speech but have been prepared to listen to others as well.

I once stood behind Mrs Thatcher as she delivered a speech. Although her speeches are delivered from a prepared script, which has often been released to the Press in advance, she was able to preface the formal parts of her presentation by humorous reference to various points made by the speakers who preceded her.

The fact that you are participating in the evening, as a whole, rather than superimposing your own isolated contribution, will add to your own enjoyment of the function. After dinner speaking should be fun and not just a dreaded duty.

2. Types of after dinner speeches

Before you even consider the preparation of a speech, it is important you are fully aware of the particular type of speech you are to make.

There are different toasts you may be asked to propose or respond to. You may be asked to speak as the principal speaker at a dinner to promote a message or cause, you may even be asked to either introduce or thank a speaker. In each case there are subtle changes of requirement in the format of your speech which will, in turn affect your subsequent preparation.

PROPOSING A TOAST

At virtually every formal dinner at least one toast is proposed and drunk by those attending. This will mean that someone is required to make a speech in proposing the toast.

The speech should be appropriate to the toast and should conclude with the actual proposal. The request for those present to join in the drinking of the toast should be succinct and simple. The old fashioned and anachronistic use of expressions like 'Please be upstanding', should be avoided. If you want the assembled guests to rise then ask them 'to stand'. When they are standing, raise your glass and propose your toast slowly and clearly. If it isn't clear enough to your audience that they should drink a toast, the toastmaster will repeat the toast for you, but this should not be necessary.

TOAST TO THE HOST ORGANIZATION

It is usual for a guest at a function (or possibly a junior member) to propose a toast to the organization responsible for the dinner.

Your hosts may be a corporate body, a social or charitable organization or even a gathering of friends and acquaintances. You may have been asked to speak as the representative of a kindred organization or as a friend of the organizers. However, the reasons for your presence as speaker are less important than what you say and how you say it. It is courtesy to your hosts to do sufficient research beforehand to enable you to compliment them and even gently pull their legs during your speech.

If you are representing a kindred organization your research should look for both the obvious parallels between your two organizations and the more apparent differences.

It is advisable to find out as much as possible about the chairman for the dinner. He is obviously, the most important of your hosts and any suitable reference to him should be included in your speech. This is an obvious courtesy but do be careful not to be sycophantic.

It is usual when a toast is proposed for a member of the host organization to respond. You should try to find out sufficient information about whoever is responding to enable you to include some suitable comment in your speech. Again, it needs research beforehand.

Remember that in proposing a toast it is presumed that you have been asked in the belief that you will be complimentary to your hosts. Your conclusion should, as a general rule, be based on this premise.

Finally you should propose the toast. As mentioned earlier this should be simple and to the point. The toast should be the one you were asked to propose. The temptation to embellish it by the addition of individuals should be avoided. A frequent error is the use of the expression, following the proper toast, of the words, 'coupled with . . .'. If the toast is to a specific organization it must be presumed that the organization is greater than the individual members. The coupling of the chairman or others' names with the proposal is both incorrect and in a way discourteous.

TOAST TO THE GUESTS

Normally a member of the host organization proposes a toast to the guests at a dinner. In this case your task is quite simply to introduce your guests to your fellow members and where necessary paint a word portrait of them.

There can be several types of guests and it is most important that you are aware of those who are present and in what capacity

Official guests The most important of your guests will be the official ones. These will probably have been invited as they are the holders of some special position or office. In researching your speech collect as much detail as possible about any official guests as they will almost certainly warrant individual reference in your address. Remember that as they are special guests, every courtesy should be extended when making reference to them and they

should never be embarrassed by any remarks you
may make.

Other important guests Next come the more
important guests who are present but have not been
invited officially. It is helpful to find out whether
there are any who fall into this category. They may
have been invited by individual members of your
organization as friends or business acquaintances.

To illustrate this sort of circumstance: I was once
present at an Institute of Bankers dinner where one
of the members had an ambassador as a personal
guest. Quite properly he warranted a mention in
the toast to the guests.

Ordinary guests At large dinners there will probably be guests of many members present who may
not deserve individual mention but should be
covered by some form of general welcome.

Do your research When doing your research for the
toast to the guests you should remember that while
there will be a number who require mention, a
catalogue of lengthy introductions can be tedious
and even boring. You will need to consider
carefully those who need individual introduction
and those who can be covered by a blanket
welcome. However, the greatest insult you can
make to an important guest is to forget to mention
him or her! This particular speech is one where
diplomacy and tact are essential.

TOASTING THE CHAIRMAN OF THE FUNCTION

This toast is, of course, a much more individual

toast and requires detailed research of the person concerned.

Try to find out as much as possible of his personal background and if possible any suitable anecdotes. Your whole approach to this speech should be based on his individual personality and the attributes that have contributed to his being appointed chairman.

Gentle teasing of the individual concerned will be acceptable but again care should always be taken not to embarrass. A fine balance between flattery and humour is the best possible mix, concluding with a suitable compliment, if possible, attributable to his chairmanship.

In all types of speeches, I have mentioned the need to avoid embarrassing any individual. This is especially true in this particular toast. To direct your humour at anyone individually, you need to know them well. If you have the slightest fear that your remarks could offend, then don't use them.

THE CIVIC TOAST

At many dinners at which the civic head of a city or town is present it is customary to propose a civic toast.

The toast would be responded to by the Lord Mayor or Mayor or other civic head. In preparing for this toast the most important area of research must be the civic community. Make sure you know enough about both the history and the current developments to be able to pay suitable tribute to both the past and the present.

You will also need to make enquiries to ensure that you are aware of the particular attributes of the current incumbent of the mayoralty.

As a general rule this is not expected to be a long and detailed speech but rather one in which you extend the courtesy of an individual welcome to the civic leader, who will normally respond to the toast.

Don't try and score points If you are proposing a civic toast you must resist any temptation to score political points even if you disagree either with the ruling local party or their methods. Remember the toast embraces all the citizens and their civic leader. For the duration of his term of office, he or she is considered impartial and non-political.

THE TOAST TO THE LADIES (OR GENTLEMEN)

At many dinners there is a toast to the ladies or gentlemen as the case may be. I suppose this is probably the most hackneyed toast of them all and one which has been proposed so often and so badly that it is difficult to think of something new to say!

Keep it simple In preparation it is essential to obtain some information about the person who will respond and to bring them into your speech. Avoid the many well worn cliches that are so often trotted out and concentrate on a simple speech. You can lace it with a little gentle humour and flattery to the opposite sex but don't use any sickly ingratiation. This is not an easy speech to make. As a general rule I would always recommend simple sincerity rather than attempting to reproduce any similar toast that you may have heard previously.

OTHER TOASTS

There are many other less usual toasts that you may

be asked to propose and each must be treated on its own merits and researched accordingly.

RESPONDING TO A TOAST

As a general rule toasts that have been proposed and drunk are usually followed by a response. If you are responding to a toast you will be in a strong position inasmuch as you will either be representing the organization to whom the toast was proposed or be the individual recipient of the toast. On the other hand, you will almost certainly have had no idea of what the proposer intended saying until you actually heard them a few moments earlier. You will, therefore, need to be able to respond to any points that he has made in an impromptu manner. Try and comment on his remarks if you can, without disrupting your own prepared response. Do however, avoid being drawn into contentious arguments over any provocative statements he may have made.

In preparing for a response your most important research must centre on the proposer. You need to both thank him and also, if necessary, to introduce him as a personality to those present. After all, they may have seen and heard him without really knowing very much about him as an individual.

RESPONDING ON BEHALF OF THE HOST ORGANIZATION

Your role in responding on behalf of the host organization must be first to thank your proposer and to tell your audience a little about him. This can include the reason for his having been invited to propose the toast. If he has done his research correctly he will already have told the guests something about your organization and care should be taken not to repeat what the proposer has already said. However, you may well be able to update his information and tell your guests of any new developments or activities that may be of interest.

The need for flexibility You can see from the above that there is a much greater need for flexibility in all cases of responding to a toast. It is so much more flattering to your proposer and interesting to your audience if you can expand on comments made in his speech.

Don't be boring The trap that so many fall into here is to bore the audience to tears with an interminable catalogue of the activities and successes of the organization.

The worst I think I ever suffered in this respect was a chairman at a dinner celebrating the twenty-fifth anniversary of his organization. His response to the toast took nearly forty-five long and boring minutes as he went through each of the twenty-five years and told us of all the personalities and happenings year by year.

RESPONDING ON BEHALF OF THE GUESTS

The first duty on responding for the guests is again to thank the proposer. However, in this case it is less likely that you will need to say a lot about him as an individual. Being one of your hosts, it is likely that he will already be well known. You may choose to make some suitably light-hearted remark about him. This will be based on the information you should have obtained beforehand, taking, as always, great care to avoid any possible offence.

If a toast has been, or will be, proposed to your hosts, there is no need to say too much about them in your speech. Indeed it would be wrong to risk repeating what has already been said or even pre-empting what might still be to come. A golden rule in preparing a speech is to try and ensure that you are not likely to conflict with any of the other speakers.

. Your basic duty is to say thank you, on behalf of your fellow guests, to your hosts for their hospitality. A sincerely expressed 'Thank you' will be as warmly received by your hosts as by your fellow guests.

RESPONDING AS CHAIRMAN

Your response in this case is to a very personal and individual toast to you. However, do not lose sight of the fact that it may have been proposed to you as the holder of a particular office and embraces that office as much as you personally.

As chairman your response is also your own opportunity to make what may well be your principal speech as holder of that office. Indeed it may be a keynote speech on behalf of your particular organization.

Almost certainly, it will also be expected that you will incorporate a number of 'thank you's' to those associated both with your organization or more specifically with the particular event.

It is very much 'your evening' but always try to resist the temptation of making too long a speech and losing the esteem you already have with your audience.

The one assurance I always give to a chairman on such occasions, is that he is the one speaker whom the audience will always support, because of his office. If, therefore, he is sensible and realistic in his presentation he will not lose that support.

RESPONDING TO OTHER TOASTS

I have already mentioned that there are many other toasts that may be proposed and many of them will demand a response.

The basic rules are similar for all responses. First, you should thank the proposer. If possible make a suitable remark about him based on the information you have obtained beforehand. Then you should attempt to complement his remarks while at the same time avoid repetition. Thirdly, if it is applicable, you should touch on any point that is relevant to your having been chosen to respond.

Be concise It is impossible not to keep stressing the need to be concise and to the point. It applies to all responses. The most eloquent of speakers never use more words than are necessary and avoid irrelevant padding in their speeches. You should always try and copy their example and never be misled into thinking that the quality of a speech is any way related to its length.

THE ROLE OF PRINCIPAL SPEAKER

There are occasions when someone is required to act as principal speaker at a dinner. This role is filled on many occasions by a paid professional speaker whose speech is an act or entertainment in itself. I would not presume to advise the professional on his approach to these occasions but will deal with the circumstances in which an amateur may be cast in the role of principal speaker.

This particular type of speech is made on an occasion with a specific purpose. The principal speaker is given an opportunity to expand on that purpose. Perhaps the dinner is in aid of a particular charity and, you, as a representative of that charity have been asked to inform the audience in the hope of encouraging their support. It may be a corporate dinner and you have been asked to project a particular message on behalf of the company.

When preparing this type of speech it is essential you consider your proposed content very carefully to ensure that it both retains and stimulates your audience. At all costs try and avoid dull and endless statistics and facts. If you need to quote figures to your audience, keep them simple and illustrate them wherever possible with day to day comparisons that they will readily appreciate and understand.

INTRODUCTION OF GUEST OR PRINCIPAL SPEAKER

There are occasions at dinners where the principal speaker is introduced to the audience by means of a short speech from a representative of the hosts.

If you are asked to make this speech it is important to obtain all the information necessary to give your speaker a full introduction. Remember you are there to whet the appetites of your audience to hear the speaker who follows. Make sure you give them a full but not fulsome background picture of him. You should make special reference to any areas of his career that caused you to invite him to speak on this occasion.

Always remember that you are there to introduce principal speaker, not to make a speech in your own right. The audience are waiting to listen to the speaker who follows and only want to hear you for as long as it takes to introduce him.

THANKING A SPEAKER

It is a courtesy to the principal or guest speakers for a member of the host organization to make a short speech of thanks.

It is flattering and observant to pick up and possibly make mention of one or maybe two points the speaker has made but the last thing the audience want to hear is a synopsis or précis of his entire speech. Indeed it is the height of discourtesy to the speaker to infer that you are having to explain his speech to his listeners! The essence of your speech is that of thanking the speaker, not of explaining him or excusing him. Remember that we are considering the situation where an amateur speaker may well have made a great effort and even a sacrifice to be with you for the evening.

The greatest compliment you can pay the speaker in your vote of thanks is for him to leave at the end of the evening feeling his efforts were truly appreciated. Even if you were not particularly impressed with the speaker's efforts, you cannot allow that to influence the thanks you are duty bound to extend to him. You can invariably find something complimentary to say about any speech.

CONCLUSION

I hope you will now begin to appreciate that there are many different types of after dinner speech. Whilst there are many similarities and the disciplines of preparation are similar, the preparation and research for each can be quite different.

It is extremely important that you are fully aware of the particular speech you have been asked to make.

In an evening of several speeches undisciplined preparation will create the danger that your contribution may conflict with that of one of the other speakers. When asked to speak make absolutely certain what other speeches are to be made and in what order. This way you can hopefully visualise the pattern of the whole evening and appreciate where you fit in the overall programme of events.

The organizers of the evening will have given careful consideration to their choice of speakers, in the belief that as a whole, they will combine to produce an enjoyable and interesting result for the guests. Bear this in mind when preparing and you will not disappoint your hosts.

3. Humour

Using humour in a speech is such an important aspect of the whole process that it warrants a chapter to itself.

There is no doubt that to listen to a speaker who is really funny is a great pleasure, but to make such a speech can be difficult.

A temptation that needs to be resisted by most speakers is trying to emulate a humorous speaker they have heard in the past. One point I always make, as strongly as possible, to any prospective speaker is to prepare a speech that is suited to him and not to attempt to copy someone else. This applies especially to humour.

Timing I have spoken elsewhere of timing in a speech and timing is all important for good humour. I remember a few years ago listening to an old, very professional, entertainer make an after dinner speech. His content was equally old, but his timing was so superb that, although most of his audience had heard his stories before, they laughed non-stop throughout his entire performance.

On the other hand I have had to listen to innumerable speakers tell funny stories that have been so badly timed that instead of providing humour they caused embarrassment to both speaker and listener.

CAN YOU HANDLE HUMOUR?

It may seem invidious to divide speakers into those who can make people laugh and those who can't. It is essential however, to think carefully before using humour. You have to be honest with yourself in deciding whether you can create laughter or not. Some people are naturally funny and are able to work humour into a speech with great skill. Others, however find it difficult to be funny and if you are one of them, admit it and resist the temptation to try. It isn't, unfortunately, the same as sharing a joke with friends.

There is a very fine line between success and failure when using humour. There is no greater feeling of success than standing up and looking around a room that is laughing and exuding happiness as a result of your speech. On the other hand there is no deeper sinking feeling in the pit of the stomach than you feel when what you believe to be your funniest material is met with stoney silence or, even worse, groans from your audience.

The final decision is yours alone, but I cannot over-emphasize the care you should exercise in making that decision. As I stressed when discussing preparation, your final presentation must be a package that will be enjoyed by the audience. You also need to be totally happy to present it to them. When considering humour do not forget these criteria.

THE DANGERS

Ideally of course any speech should avoid offending even a single member of the audience. In trying to be funny this is particularly relevant.

Broad humour In after dinner speeches doubtful or dubious jokes should be avoided at all costs. The type of humour that is enjoyed by a group of men in the bar is often quite unsuitable for a speech. I am old fashioned enough to believe that in spite of this great modern move to equality of the sexes, the use of broad or raunchy humour when speaking to mixed audiences is wrong. It is an insult to the intelligence of those listening and many would consider it impolite to the opposite sex. Therefore it must always be a risk that someone listening may be offended, if not for themselves, possibly for the sake of others.

Bad language The use of expletives or bad language, even to single sex audiences, should also be totally avoided. There are those who believe that they can obtain laughs by shocking their audience. My own view is that it indicates a lack of preparation, a sad deficiency in vocabulary, or plain bad taste.

Never risk offence in the hope of obtaining cheap laughs.

REMEMBER WHY YOU ARE SPEAKING

If you are contemplating being bold and going for a humorous after dinner speech do not forget the reason you were asked to speak in the first place. I have heard numerous speakers who have been invited to propose a toast at a particular function, and have decided to make a funny speech. In doing so they have forgotten the whole purpose of their presence and have finished up by proposing the relevant toast almost as an afterthought. This is basically an insult to your hosts.

If you have decided to be funny, then remember the difficulties in balancing your humour with the *raison d'être* of your speech. Most of you will not have been engaged as stand-up comics. To trot out story after story, however funny they may be, without any relevance to the speech you were invited to make is a danger that should be avoided. The really good humorous after dinner speaker will use relatively few stories as such but they will have been tailored and adapted to have some relevance to the particular occasion. As a result he will receive the compliments of his audience and the thanks of his hosts for the obvious care in preparation for what is undoubtedly their special occasion.

WHAT TYPE OF HUMOUR?

There are so many different types of humour and the use of them is almost as personal as the choice of clothes you wear. As one who tries to be funny after dinner, I know that I hear others telling stories that however funny and well received they may be, are quite unsuited to my own style. On the other hand I have heard stories that have failed dismally, gone away and thought about them, adapted them and subsequently used them very successfully. Remember you would be an exceptional speaker if you could use all types of humour. Try and decide what is your particular style, then stick to it and work hard until you have perfected it.

Accepting that there is very little original humour, all of us rely on what we have heard or seen in different situations to provide the basis for being funny. There are some stories which stand entirely on their own being very funny but do not lend themselves to adaptation. However good they may be if they are totally irrelevant to the occasion then I would recommend that you do not use them. There are others that are very general in content that can easily be adapted to suit specific occasions.

The use of humour requires more preparation than any other content in your speech.

THE ONE-LINER

I am a great believer in the use of the one-liner as a form of humour in speeches.

There are obvious merits in this type of humour. It is short, which in itself is an advantage. Speakers who tell long stories can on occasions be sufficiently nervous or distracted by a noise in the audience to lose their place and make a mistake that can ruin the story; not so with the one-liner. It is quick and it is less hazardous from a memory point of view. It also has the advantage that if it fails it is in itself a very small part of the speech as a whole. It is also almost impossible for those who have heard it already to pre-empt the finish because it is over so quickly.

The one-liner also has the merit that it can usually be very easily adapted and angled towards a personality present which at least gives the impression that you have gone to some trouble to do your homework for the occasion.

THE LONG STORY

Of course, jokes or stories, like people, come in all shapes and sizes. Long stories are among the hardest to use.

If you are trying to tell a lengthy story with an ultimate punch-line, beware! Assuming you have a reasonable number in the audience there will almost certainly be a percentage who will know the story you are telling and may well reach the end before you do. If they do so in silence there is little problem. If however, they decide to tell their neighbours they will certainly kill it for you with that part of the audience. It is therefore essential if you decide to tell a long and involved story, you tell it well. You need to have rehearsed it time and again to yourself to ensure that your timing is as near perfect as you can make it and that you are able to wring every last ounce of humour from it.

It is even better if you can adapt the longer story to embrace a personality present, someone who is not likely to be offended by your doing so. What is more, you can present it in a more raconteur style than as a straightforward joke.

DIRECTING HUMOUR TO INDIVIDUALS PRESENT

When setting out to prepare a speech in which you aim to be funny, it is as well to find out as much as you can about personalities among your hosts or your guests. This can usually be achieved by a direct approach to whoever invited you to speak in the first place or by contacting anyone you know associated with the organization involved.

Great care must be taken when involving individuals especially if you do not know them personally. I will repeat again that it is absolutely essential that you avoid offending any single person present.

Remember that your audience will laugh with the person you have decided to involve in your humour, but they will never laugh against them if they feel that there is any danger that he or she may be offended. Gentle leg-pulling is the result you should be trying to achieve as opposed to barbed or pointed humour at someone's expense.

Most people enjoy being mentioned in a speech even if it is in a humorous way so handled properly this type of approach can indeed win you friends in the audience.

SO SHOULD YOU TRY AND BE FUNNY?

Very early in this book I suggested that people attending a dinner where there were to be after dinner speeches were hoping to be entertained rather than sit through a series of lectures. I expressed the belief that even if speeches, of necessity, had to contain serious points, they did not need to be dull. In this context the use of humour must be a very important tool in any good speaker's armoury.

That humour must be tailored to your own ability and capability to present it in an acceptable and agreeable manner. As in all aspects of after dinner speaking you must know your own limitations and play to your strengths. Avoid over-reaching your-self and attempting forms of humour in which you have no confidence or belief. Unless you are as near certain as possible that you will get 'the laugh' forget it!

Use your humour sparingly and relevantly. If you have two or three good, appropriate, humorous comments that you can work into your speech then don't pad it out with other jokes just for the sake of trying to introduce more humour. Remember if you are not convinced that a particular comment is especially funny, others certainly will not!

4. Preparing your speech

Having listened to thousands of speeches as a toastmaster I would suggest that the principal reason for the high percentage of poor speeches is lack of proper preparation. I am often surprised by people, frequently in senior positions in business or society, who seem to believe that just by standing up and opening their mouths they will be able to make a memorable speech.

There is no short cut to avoid proper preparation. No actor can portray a part successfully unless he has both learnt his lines and rehearsed them well. Similarly, no speaker can make a good speech unless he has prepared it well. He needs to become so familiar with it that he has complete confidence in what he is going to say before he rises to his feet.

Practice may not make perfect but it can certainly go a long way towards it. There is no golden rule for the amount of time it takes to prepare a speech. Some people can assemble their ideas more quickly than others. Others can absorb their notes more quickly. The length of time you must spend depends on how long it takes to be confident in the knowledge that you have prepared a speech you are happy to deliver. If you have any doubts, then try to make more time available to continue your preparation.

ESTABLISH THE BASICS

Begin your preparation by listing the known facts about your speech. This may seem over-simplification but there are many occasions when I am sure a speaker has prepared his address without any real consideration of the brief he must have been given.

The purpose of the occasion First of all, are you proposing a toast or responding to one? It will have been seen from the previous chapter that there are basic differences between the two.

Secondly, what is the occasion on which you are to speak? This will determine whether your speech needs to be of a rather more serious nature in its content or whether you can take a slightly more informal and humorous approach.

The importance of time Thirdly, for how long are you to speak? If you are not sure – then ask. You must know this before you start. So many speeches have rambled on to the embarrassment of both the audience and the hosts that one can only assume the speakers either had no brief in this respect or chose to ignore it!

There was an occasion which will always remain a classic in my memory. A member of the Royal Family was present and the speaker before them must have been given a specific amount of time for his speech. Given the tight schedule so often involved with the Royal Family it was only about five minutes. After ten minutes, subtle messages were passed to the speaker who deliberately ignored them all. After fifteen minutes an exasperated organizer walked straight up to the speaker and placed a note in front of him which read, quite simply, 'Sit down'. The speaker still spoke for a further five minutes before concluding!

The speaker was in fact a very well known broadcaster who should have known better. The

effect was considerable embarrassment to all concerned and a very poor reception for the speech.
This is, of course, an extreme example but I hope it
illustrates the fact that you should always stick to
your brief for time. To do so, you must know the
time required before you even start preparing. As a
rule it is always safer to be a little under your time
than to exceed it.

In this particular respect you are very much on
trust; it is unlikely that anyone will physically
attempt to stop you speaking once you have started
– please don't let them wish they could!

The other speakers Finally, in establishing the basic
requirements of your speech, it is useful to check
how many speakers precede or follow you.

If there are several speakers before you, you will
want to know something of the speeches they are
going to make. This will help you avoid repeating
anything which has already been said. It is not an
unusual occurrence when there are several speeches
at a dinner to find that each successive speaker is
tending to some extent to repeat what his pre-
decessor has been saying. The result is that each
speaker becomes less interesting and less likely to
have any hold on his audience. I shall deal later
with flexibility in your speech. This is very necessary if you are faced with the problem that most of
your best points or jokes having been used by those
speaking before you.

It is equally necessary to have an idea of those
who will follow. If there are a number still to come
after you it makes sticking to your time brief even
more important. It also helps you to ensure that
your own contribution is not likely to detract from a
speech to be made later in the proceedings.

On an evening of numerous speeches remember, you are one of a team to entertain your listeners, not a competitor in a speaking competition!

THINK ABOUT YOUR SPEECH

Once you have satisfied yourself on the basic parameters of your speech (and I would suggest you write them down) you are ready to begin preparing it.

Very few people are capable of saying 'I will sit down on Sunday afternoon after lunch and write a speech'. Most of us will need to give it considerable thought before writing. In my opinion this thinking period is possibly the most important part of the preparation process. All of us have time during our waking day to think. I find that travel is an excellent time for thinking, be it by public transport or while driving my car.

The other period of time I find most productive is that time between resting my head on the pillow and actually falling asleep. My wife always comments that rather than count sheep, I mentally rehearse openings and closing of speeches and, of course, my impromptus!

When you feel that you have enough ideas in your mind to commit yourself to the first draft then is the time to write and not before. You may, as I suggested earlier, keep notes but don't try and put it in a final form until you have a fairly clear idea in your mind of the overall form it will take.

BREAK YOUR SPEECH DOWN INTO PARTS

Any speech must comprise a number of parts. As a simple rule it can be broken down into the beginning, the middle and the ending or closing. This may sound almost over-simplification but it is vital that they are treated as quite separate components which make a complete entity when finally put together.

The beginning When you stand for the start of your speech the most important requirement is to attract the attention of your audience. Your initial impact will create an instant reaction among your listeners. Will they like what you are about to say or not! Prepare the start of your speech with short positive sentences. If you start with rambling long-winded sentences you will almost certainly lack conviction. Remember that you want to start with your audience believing they want to listen to you. Avoid all the well worn cliches all of us have heard so often at the beginning of speeches and never, ever, apologize for either speaking or for what you are about to say. If you are saying sorry almost before you begin, the audience are hardly likely to feel inspired to concentrate on the rest of what you have to say.

The middle This is the main part of your speech. Having gained your audience's attention with your opening remarks and prepared them for what is the real purpose of your speech, you can now proceed with your central theme.

Your research should have ensured that there is no doubt in your own mind as to the purpose of the speech. Make sure your content is totally appropriate to your brief and avoid any irrelevant deviation. If you are to inform your audience in any way make your points clearly and precisely. Avoid at all costs long and boring lists of facts or statistics that are difficult for the listeners to absorb. Be sympathetic to your listener in preparing this part of your speech. A good criterion is to read through what you have written and be honest with yourself; would it interest you if you were to have to listen to it? So often I feel speakers adopt a rather selfish attitude in presuming that because a very detailed explanation of a given subject interests them, then it must interest their audience.

The closing Sometimes the hardest part of making a speech on any occasion is to know when and how to finish.

Just as the initial impact of your opening remarks will have ensured an attentive audience, so the end of your speech should leave them with the sensation of having enjoyed your presentation and a clear understanding of your point of view.

Where your central theme has contained an important message it may be wise to include a short paraphrase of your remarks. This must be very short and to the point as no audience wants to listen to you repeating a large proportion of what you have already said.

Obviously if you are in the fortunate position of proposing a toast you have an obvious conclusion to your speech. If you are responding to a toast or making some other form of speech try and leave them with a smile or even a suitable closing provocative thought.

Remember that the greatest tribute your listeners can pay is to say that you sat down with them wanting more – avoid the temptation of giving it to them!

PREPARING TO WRITE IT OUT IN FULL

Having collected your thoughts (or notes) into the various sections of your speech now is the time to write it out in full.

I do not believe that a speaker should, as a rule, speak from a fully written script but I do consider it very good discipline to begin by writing a full and extended draft.

Rules for a good speech There are certain rules to remember in writing your first draft.

Spoken not written As I said before many speakers forget when writing a speech that there is a very positive difference between the written and the spoken word. A successfully-delivered speech should sound as if it is a conversational piece, between the speaker and his audience. If it is prepared and learnt as a purely written exercise it will have the effect of sounding rather stilted when delivered, almost like reading a letter out aloud. This can have the effect on the listener of his feeling that you are talking 'at him' rather than 'to him'.

USE GOOD ENGLISH

Although you should make your speech 'conversational', it should still be good English.

Our language is a delightful one when used properly. Sir Winston Churchill's great speeches illustrate how effective good English can be. Some people are tempted, however, to use slang or corrupt expressions and even, on occasions bad language to try and make their points.

It is a pity when speakers resort to this and I can only exhort you to avoid it at all costs. An audience will be more impressed and less likely to be offended if the language is good.

If your speech is constructed with due care and attention to the use of the language, it will certainly flow better. It will be easier to memorize and be more acceptably pleasing to the ear of the listener. It will also flatter your hosts to believe that your speech is soundly constructed, rather than giving the impression of having been thrown together at the last moment.

WRITE IN SECTIONS INITIALLY

The opening section Your opening section needs to make quick impact and should immediately keep your audience's attention.

The sentences you prepare for this stage should be very clear in their content and particularly easy for you to deliver. When you first rise to your feet you will almost certainly feel nervous. You need to ease yourself into your stride. I will deal more fully with the question of delivery a little later, but it is important that you are aware of the dangers. By writing long sentences or using long or unfamiliar words you will only add to the strain of those opening moments. To begin by stumbling over your opening sentences will make your audience embarrassed for you and even sympathetic. This is not the impact you want to make.

If you envisage using a joke or humorous comment in your opening, write it out in full at this stage. Humour needs almost more care and rehearsal than any other part of your content. (For further details, see *Humour*, pp. 36–42.)

The main section It is a good idea to start by listing various points you feel you want to make. Having done so, read through them and make sure there is nothing you have omitted. Equally essential, make sure there is nothing irrelevant on the list.

Now put the list of points into a logical order. There is nothing worse than a speaker who jumps from point to point in no sensible sequence and at times appears to be making his points almost as afterthoughts. There is little sense in preparing your main theme, which presumably you would like the audience to remember and retain, if you present it to them as an illogically ordered hotch-potch!

Having worked out a sequence of points write it all out, avoiding long dull or statistical passages wherever possible. Remember it is extremely difficult to deliver anything with any sort of conviction if you are not happy with it yourself. If you have doubts about any of your points and your ability to project them to your audience, put them on one side at this stage. It will be easier to rethink them later if you feel they are a vital part of your message.

Write your closing The finish should carry the same sort of punch as the opening did. It needs the same short positive sentences.

If you wish to reiterate the main point of your central theme use no more than a couple of very short sentences. Above all make sure that you use different phraseology. No one wants to hear a repetition of your points word for word, a change of wording may well add impact.

If you finish with the proposal of a toast, make that proposal clear and positive. As mentioned earlier do not embellish or alter the toast you have been given. If you have any doubt as to the exact wording of the toast ask the toastmaster for his advice and he will be happy to help you.

If you are not proposing a toast do try to construct a form of wording that gives a positive conclusion to your speech. A speech that appears to peter out and is only obviously concluded because the speaker has sat down, is very unlikely to leave the audience with any lasting memories! That final impact is arguably the fine line between the really successful speaker and the more ordinary, and more forgettable, one!

EDITING

Having written a first draft you should consider it objectively, realizing that it is only the beginning. It is going to need editing, reconsidering and rewriting. The time that you are prepared to spend on this could be the most significant contributory factor to the ultimate success of your speech.

Be ruthless Any approach to editing must be ruthless. If you are not prepared to accept second best from yourself then there is a fair chance that your audience will hear the best that you could give them. Your final aim must be to have at your command a speech with which you are totally happy and at ease. It will almost come to feel like an old friend even before you have delivered it.

Editing has to be like pruning the roses in your garden, the harder you cut them back, the better they grow. The harder you prune your draft, the more positive and suitable the phrases you put in. You can only achieve this by total honesty with yourself – it's a great exercise in self discipline!

Read it out aloud Take yourself into some quiet corner with your first draft and read it aloud to yourself, just as you have prepared it. Time yourself, allowing for pauses and laughs, speaking slowly and clearly.

You will be an exceptional person if you are totally happy with the result!

Did you like it as a speech? Having read it could you honestly say you liked it? Some parts will sound quite good. Be frank with yourself but try and analyse the points you did not like. Note down the most obvious changes you feel are necessary to the basic content. The aim is to make it more acceptable to you, and easier to deliver.

Did you believe in it? Having read it and placed yourself in the position of your audience, did you believe in what you were trying to say? Did you believe it was sincere and honest? There is no substitute for sincerity in a speaker. Nor is there anything more patently transparent than a lack of it.

How was the timing? How did the time compare with the time you had been allocated?

If it was too short you need to consider whether it would be advisable to leave it short in the knowledge that it covers all you wished to say. You could extend it by adding back in some of the ideas that you originally omitted. Do not lengthen it by the use of irrelevant padding – far better to leave it short.

If it was too long (which is more likely the case) then you will need to edit out material. Check that you are not using twelve words where two would do! Have you repeated yourself at all?

Remember be ruthless with yourself especially on this first run through. No one else can be.

WILL IT SOUND AS GOOD AS IT READS?

If you have been totally honest with yourself in this first run through then you will probably have spotted odd phrases or sentences that do not sound quite right as you read them.

Mark these problem areas and consider how you would normally express yourself when speaking, as opposed to writing. In many instances the change of a single word will make it sound better. In other cases you may well need to re-write a whole sentence. Never be afraid to re-write whole sections to achieve a result that is pleasing to you.

If as it becomes more easily conversational it begins to give you pleasure, then you are much more likely to be able to communicate that pleasure to the listening audience.

The optimum is to finish with sentences and words that trip off your tongue; sentences that are well constructed, good English and sound and feel perfectly natural to you as you speak them.

TIME TO RE-WRITE

Having had your first run through you should now re-write your draft incorporating all your various amendments.

Maybe you are now beginning to wonder whether all this effort is worth it. Your first efforts are bound to take a bit longer. Let us presume that you are planning to speak for about fifteen minutes. Putting it all into perspective, have you really spent long so far? Isn't it worthwhile to do the job thoroughly? I suppose one of the driving factors in our time and effort is our personal pride. No one ever wants to stand and make a speech that he knows will fail even before he starts. This preparation must be time well spent.

Having re-written the draft, try it out again. You will almost certainly find that many of the prolems have disappeared and further amendments are far fewer. Continue rehearsing your speech aloud whenever the opportunity arises and gradually you will begin to feel that no further adjustments are necessary. In fact, you will find you have committed a good deal of it to memory. Soon you will realize that you have really got a speech that is going to be worth listening to!

NOW TO START LEARNING IT

Learning your speech doesn't mean committing every word to memory.

What you will in fact do is create a working knowledge of its contents. You need to familiarize yourself with the sequence of the various points that you are making and the particular phraseology that you have decided to use. As I said earlier, your audience would not enjoy sitting and watching you read a speech so this is a very important stage.

COMMITTING IT TO NOTE FORM

At the same time as learning the basic content you should start reducing your speech to note form. Notes generally should be restricted to headings and lead words. These notes are intended as a support for your speech and should be prepared, so that you can read them easily, when necessary.

Lead words, are key words to remind you of a particular point, comment or joke that you are intending to use. A glance at the word in your notes will automatically jog your brain and lead you into that part of your speech. You won't need to have written extensive notes.

Use of cards for notes The best method of having your final notes to hand while you speak is to put them on cards. A postcard or something similar is ideal. The cards should be carefully numbered and preferably joined together in a top corner by a treasury tag or similar fixing so that they are easy to turn over.

Remember they are only of use to you if you can read them! Print them in letters of sufficient size to see them at a glance. You can also highlight specific points with a marker.

The advantage of cards is that they are easy to handle and carry in your pocket or handbag and that much tougher than paper. They are also less obtrusive when you are giving your speech.

The most important point is to have some form of prompt available. This will give you both support and confidence while speaking. Hopefully it will ensure that you are able to make your speech flow as a whole, without stopping and starting as you search for the next sentence. Always make life as easy as you can for yourself.

If you really feel the need to have your speech written out in full in front of you, then you should do so. The more comfortable and happy you are about your supporting notes the easier your speech will be. Here again you should mark the pages so that it is easy to find your place when you glance down.

FAMILIARITY

Once you have committed your final draft to the form that you intend to use on the evening, take every opportunity to familiarize yourself with your speech.

The more you read, remember, recite or think about the speech the more like an old friend it will become. If you feel you are completely familiar with what you are going to say, so you will become more confident about it and less nervous as the day approaches.

ALL THAT'S LEFT NOW IS TO DELIVER IT!

Having prepared your best possible speech, let us consider how you intend to deliver it!

Delivery is all important to your final impact on your audience and in the next chapter I will deal extensively with the art of delivering a good speech. It would be a sin to prepare a good speech and then spoil it when you rise to your feet.

5. Preparing yourself

You have prepared for most eventualities now but have you prepared yourself?

How you feel when you stand to speak will have a considerable bearing on how you actually perform. Remember it is a performance you are about to give in the same way that any entertainer performs to his audience.

CHECK THE DRESS

Make absolutely sure you know the dress that is expected for the evening. It is usual for the ticket to specify the dress. However, if you are a guest who has been invited to speak it is quite likely that you will not have a ticket. If you arrive at what is an evening dress occasion in a lounge suite or its female equivalent, you will be both embarrassed and considerably disadvantaged – especially if you are too far from home to be able to rectify the error.

DON'T DELIBERATELY OVER OR UNDER DRESS

Having established the correct dress, try to compliment the guests by dressing accordingly. Do not try and create an effect by deliberately over or under dressing. This is a discourtesy to your hosts and could well backfire when it comes to your speech.

I was once present at a dinner jacket function at which the principal speaker deliberately appeared in casual clothes to underline his political disagreement with his hosts. Good speaker though he was, he lost any respect he might have had before he even started.

As I said earlier in the book, the audience does not have to agree with the speaker to respect him or her, so why deliberately risk losing any of that respect.

THINK ABOUT THE DAY AS A WHOLE IN ADVANCE

If you know you are going to speak on a particular evening, try to plan a reasonably relaxed day to precede it. Avoid contentious meetings, if possible, strenuous physical activities that could leave you tired are also to be avoided, heavy and over-indulgent lunches are right out! If you are comfortably relaxed it is much better than fighting off the rigours of the preceding hours of stress.

TIMING FOR THE EVENING

Make quite certain of the timing for the evening. Know the time you are expected to arrive and make the necessary allowances to arrive early rather than late.

Arriving early will enable you to make the necessary helpful checks of the geography of the room and the microphones. If you have some distance to travel, make all the necessary allowances for any possible rush hour delays. To arrive early and relaxed is infinitely more conducive to a good performance than to arrive late and flustered.

CHECK THE TIME ALLOWED FOR YOUR SPEECH

Make certain that you and your hosts or organizers agree on the time allowed for your speech.

Circumstances can change and that may lead to the organizers asking you to shorten your time to allow them to introduce an additional item to the proceedings. If possible always co-operate and help them. It won't be too difficult to trim your speech if necessary but I would advise most speakers to resist a request to extend their prepared speech. It could mean using material that lacks that familiarity your prepared speech has, and as a result it might prove difficult to put over with the same conviction as your prepared speech.

ON ARRIVAL

Your first duty must be to let your hosts know that you have arrived. This is not only courteous but also serves to put their minds at rest.

Having done this, quietly excuse yourself and go and physically check the room in which you are to speak. If there is a toastmaster make yourself known to him and seek his help and guidance. He should be able to tell you where you are sitting. Go to the exact seat and stand behind your chair and ask the simple question – can everyone in the room see me? If the answer is 'No' then see if there is a convenient, visible spot to which you could move when the time comes.

Get the feel of the room, consider where your attention needs to be focused. Are there any great empty spaces which do not need to be directly addressed? Is there more than one level to which you need to adjust your sight line? Make sure that you feel you know the room so that when you stand up you are happy about it, it is invariably too late when you get to your feet to realize you are not going to be comfortable where you are.

CHECK THE EQUIPMENT

Next familiarize yourself with the microphone; check the height and how to adjust it. Check whether there is an 'on' and 'off' switch, so often speakers start with the microphone switched off, not noticing it in their nervousness until someone has had to interrupt to draw their attention to the mistake. The other danger with switches is the risk of accidentally switching off while speaking, if you fiddle with the microphone.

If you need a lectern now is the time to enquire if one is available. Failing that decide what alternative method you can employ for your notes. If the venue has a lectern but have not put it out, an early request will avoid any last minute panic.

When you rise to speak there is no substitute for that feeling of confidence to be gained from knowing that you have checked all your equipment and props and that you know how they work and indeed that they are working.

While you will have total control of yourself, it is always as well to check all the inanimate objects yourself and not relying on someone else's word. Always try and retain as much control of your own destiny as possible.

CHECK THE MENU

You know what you have already been told is the speech that you are making, now is the time to check that the menu says the same! Mistakes can happen.

I have known someone attend a dinner believing that he was proposing the health of the host organization only to find that on the printed menu he was replying for the guests. Obviously this is a rare and unusual discrepancy but should it happen the earlier it is discovered the more time there is to make the necessary adjustments to your speech.

In checking the menu you will obtain the first indication of the likely preamble you will need to make to your speech. Again this is an area in which the toastmaster's help is invaluable. As toastmasters are not always engaged I will set out a few simple guidelines for preambles.

PREAMBLE

This is the preface to your speech, which extends your courtesy to those important people present. You will nearly always start 'Mr Chairman' (or 'Mr President') or its feminine equivalent. It would normally then be enough to use the all embracing phrases 'Distinguished guests, ladies and gentlemen'. Never forget to preamble your speech. Not to do so is a discourtesy to those present which should always be avoided.

Avoid the temptation to include too many in the preamble. It should be kept as short and correct as possible. Do not worry yourself too much over the protocol of the preamble. Unless you are the first speaker those who go before will have given you a lead. If you are first and there are those important enough to mention you can be sure the organizers will have made the necessary enquiries for the benefit of their own speakers. A quick word with them will soon provide you with the necessary information.

Make a note of any names you need to mention, making quite sure you know how to pronounce any unusual names.

DON'T OVER-INDULGE

Your speech will usually be at a congenial and sociable occasion so your hosts will be anxious that their hospitality is not found wanting. You will need to be careful to moderate your indulgence.

It is very important to make sure that you retain full use of all your faculties in readiness for your speech. Senses that have been gently but steadily dulled as the evening wears on are not conducive to a good speech. On one hand there is the very positive danger of problems of delivery, with slurring and completely uncoordinated timing. On the other is the possibility of losing your way in your train of thought and as a result rambling. A few years ago I had to listen to a speaker who had imbibed a considerable amount of what he considered to be 'Dutch courage'. The first couple of minutes were quite funny. The next couple were mildly funny but the remaining fifteen, while his wife and his friends desperately tried to get him to finish, were distinctly embarrassing to all concerned.

Remember once you are up and speaking the one person who must have total control of the situation is you. A clear thinking mind is essential to ensure that you achieve and maintain that objective.

6. Delivering your speech

You can probably remember occasions when you have lost interest in a speaker. How often have you wished a speaker would finish and sit down? Far more often, I would suggest, than you have sat and hoped the speaker would continue a little longer, because you were so enjoying his presentation. The aim here is to help you belong to the latter category.

I earlier talked of trying to place yourself in the position of your audience, and I believe this is very important in considering the delivery of the speech. You do need to give as much thought to how you are going to handle yourself when you start speaking, as you do to your preparation of the words themselves.

Preparation and presentation are the two ends of the sequence of events involved in speech making. They can never be divorced one from the other. Indeed, however good one is, without the other it is nothing!

STARTING YOUR SPEECH

In dealing with the preparation of the speech, I said how important a good start was, to enable you to begin by getting your audience on your side. This is equally important as far as your personal presentation is concerned. No matter how good your opening words are, you must get them over to the listener.

My advice to beginners is always to take their time at the start. Do not leap to your feet and launch into your speech and give an apparent indication of your delight in the opportunity to get it over with!

Once you have been introduced, usually by the toastmaster, take a slow deep breath and slowly rise to your feet. Make sure first that whoever is making the introduction knows exactly who you are and why you have been chosen to speak so that you are not put at a disadvantage before you start speaking. Having risen, make sure your position is comfortable and place your notes where you can see them easily. Make certain you are happy with the microphone position and if you need spectacles – put them on! Then and only then, start speaking.

Above all start speaking slowly. This does not mean using a dull slow monotone but it does mean don't start by swallowing your opening sentences at a speed that gives your audience no chance to hear them. It is quite true that it takes the human ear a few seconds to adjust to a new voice. Give your audience that opportunity.

THE VOICE

I am amazed at times by the apparently false voices that many speakers assume when called upon to speak in public. The voice that you can handle best and the one you are most used to, is your own!

Try to speak as normally as possible. Do not attempt a false accent. It is worth bearing in mind in every aspect of after dinner speaking that if you are comfortable in your own presentation, your audience will be equally comfortable in listening to you. As I keep emphasizing you should, at all times, make it as easy as possible for the listener.

It is essential that your audience can hear every word whether there is a microphone or not. This may mean that at times you will need to project your voice to help the listener. Voice projection does not mean shouting, this is as hard to the ear as straining to hear. True projection comes from breathing properly and slowly and bringing the voice from lower down towards the stomach and not forcing it from the throat. It is something else that you can practise beforehand when on your own, in the bath or in the car. You will soon learn how to breath to create the best projection.

TIMING

When you speak in general conversation, you take numerous pauses and breath quite naturally, you certainly don't even think about it. So it should be when speaking formally, which is only an extension of conversation. It is strange how many speakers change their conversational timing when speaking in public.

The most common fault when speakers rise is the tendency to speak faster than usual. This is why it is so important to learn to breath normally. In breathing and pausing naturally our speech will become more conversational and easier to the ear of the listener.

The use of the pause itself is too often over-looked. It is a particularly useful tool in adding emphasis to a point or in accentuating humour.

It is frequently only the nervous panic that overtakes speakers that causes them to rush through the words in a totally unnatural manner. By slowing down, especially at the start, and consciously trying to breath normally, your whole presentation will appear so much more natural and pleasing to the audience.

In finalizing your preparation do give very positive thought to the timing of your delivery and practise this thoroughly.

DO NOT DISTRACT YOUR AUDIENCE

Once you have started your speech try and handle yourself in a normal and relaxed manner. There are several irritating habits that appear to creep up and overtake speakers to the complete distraction of the listening audience.

STAND UP

Stand comfortably to your normal height. If you are having to stoop to speak you look awkward. There are various likely reasons for doing this. You may feel that you must do so to speak into the microphone. If that is the case then you should have ensured that the microphone was the right height for you when you first stood up. Perhaps you have difficulty in reading your notes. If that is so, then you should have either written them in bolder script or if a lectern is available you should place them on it. If there is no lectern, try putting your notes on top of a glass to raise them if you don't want to hold them yourself.

If you look uncomfortable your audience will feel sorry for you and this is not the reaction you were seeking from them. As I have repeated frequently, if you are not comfortable you are placing an unnecessary strain on yourself.

STAND STILL

It is so much easier to listen to a fairly static speaker than it is to have to keep re-focusing to keep up with him!

This is not as facetious a statement as you may think. An inability to stand still is a fault that quite a few speakers display. Quite often it is one they do not realize they are doing and are quite surprised when it is pointed out to them.

There are speakers who start to either sway from side to side, or rock backwards and forwards on their heels whilst standing and speaking. A predictable reaction from some members of the audience is to stop listening to the words and to begin to wonder at what point the speaker will actually lose his balance and fall over! This is not a habit most of us have in normal conversation and it really should be avoided at all costs when speaking. As I said earlier, when you first stand up, make sure you are comfortable before you start. If you feel the need to adjust your position during your speech, make your move a positive and natural one and do not spend your time moving around to the annoyance of your audience.

Your audience want to be as relaxed and comfortable too. Do not make them uncomfortable by moving around unnecessarily.

DON'T FIDGET

Having adopted a comfortable standing position do not spoil it by constant fidgetting while you speak.

There are several common forms of fidgetting you should try and avoid. There is the 'tidy' speaker who is overcome with an irresistible urge to rearrange any cutlery, china or glass that remains on the table in front of him!

Next is the 'affluent' speaker, obviously male as a rule, who insists on counting rather noisily the loose change in his pocket. There are those of us who are listening who attempt to count it with him and even take bets on the ultimate total!

Then we have the 'key' speaker who rattles the keys in his pocket to the point that we feel if he is that keen to leave the sooner he finishes and does so the better.

There are a number of other variations, all of which can only distract your audience. Do try and avoid these habits at all costs.

The occasional movement won't matter but do try and avoid letting them become irritating habits. If you do fidget because you are nervous it should improve as you go but in the meantime try and find a way of stopping yourself.

HANDS

All of us have hands at the end of our arms and when some people speak their hands assume enormous proportions and all their attempts to hide them fail, they are all you are conscious of.

The hands often seem the hardest part of the body to control.

Speakers who gesticulate incessantly with their hands only distract the listener and add little to their presentation. There are occasions when a gesture would indeed add emphasis to a point but this will be destroyed if you have been using them all the time. As a general rule hands should remain still whilst speaking.

Depending on your height you may be able to put a hand on the table but make sure you don't stoop to do so or look as though you are leaning on the table.

If you have a lectern in front of you you may find it helps to rest your hands gently on either side of it. If you are holding your notes then at least this will ensure that one hand remains occupied, as will be the case if you are holding the microphone. Otherwise place your hands comfortably at your side and leave them there. Do not put your hands in your pockets. Apart from the temptation to then play with the contents of your pocket, it looks untidy and slovenly.

SPECTACLES

Those who wear reading glasses naturally put them on when they need them and take them off when they don't. Why then I often wonder do speakers who wear glasses spend so much time playing with them?

Frequently a speaker will appear to spend his time putting them on and taking them off to the point where we begin to wonder, and even to try and work out for ourselves, what particular circumstances really require him to wear them.

I actually once watched someone who spoke for over thirty minutes during which time he had a pair of glasses in his hand, which he never put on once, not even when he referred to his notes. I was so fascinated I forgot what he was talking about!

If you wear glasses use them only as needed and do not allow them to become a source of distraction to your audience.

Remember that our eyes are often first drawn to look at anything by a movement. If that movement is irrelevant then our attention will be distracted.

OTHER DISTRACTING HABITS

Give some serious thoughts to any habits that you feel may creep into your presentation if they could distract your audience from what you are saying to them.

I have pointed out a few of the more obvious mannerisms in this respect. Most of them can be overcome if you are honest with yourself in your preparation. If you know you have a habit that may be a problem practise to eradicate it from your final presentation.

Under this heading you must include the difficult habit of using words like 'Um' and 'Er'. Some people use them in place of pauses or perhaps because they have lost their place. Knowing your speech well or being able to find your place easily in your notes will help you avoid getting into the habit. Also make sure you don't keep repeating expressions or phrases. They could prove irritating.

I once counted a speaker use the expression 'in actual fact' over twenty times in ten minutes. Many of us have habits of this type without realizing it, but it is another area where good preparation can overcome a problem. You just need to be honest with yourself and work to deal with any tendency to over-use such phrases.

I am not a great advocate of the use of tape-recorders in speech preparation but it can be useful to use one for a trial run of your speech. It may frighten you to hear your voice as others hear it, if you have not done so before. It will also highlight any irritating repetitious habits you may have.

MICROPHONES

A microphone is often an essential piece of equipment when speaking and a helpful tool particularly in a large venue though it can present problems if you are not used to using one.

As I said earlier, when you rise to speak make sure you are comfortable and this includes being happy with the microphone. Just a few seconds spent adjusting it will avoid your trying to bend or stretch to use it. You will, as I suggested earlier, have already tried it out for height and sound but the previous speaker may well have needed it a different height to you.

It helps to bear in mind certain things about microphones when you come to use one for the first time.

Microphones are directional Many microphones will only amplify the sound of your voice when you speak directly into them.

The obvious problem here is that if the microphone is fixed and you start moving your head to bring your audience, or individual members of them, into your speech you may be losing volume. It is very distracting to listen to a speaker who is rising and falling in volume as he moves his head from side to side.

Personally, I always prefer to hold a microphone in my hand. That way if I turn my head, so long as my arm moves in unison, the microphone is always in front of my mouth. I realise that many speakers feel that they would rather keep the microphone on its stand but in that case you must be careful not to move your head around too much.

Microphones can be very sensitive Remember that a microphone will not only amplify your words, but also your actions. Do not play with a static microphone during your speech by touching it, this can cause interference.

If you are holding a microphone you probably won't have this kind of trouble but you can always make sure when you do your pre-speech check.

Microphone stands are adjustable If the microphone is on a stand, once you have adjusted it you should then leave it alone.

I have seen speakers on so many occasions leaning on the microphone while speaking and as a result lowering it to below the height they had set it. The speaker then has to struggle to return it to its proper height. Apart from distracting the audience, this can be very unsettling to the speaker.

Volume A microphone, by definition, is to improve the volume of your voice to the benefit of the listener. Some microphones however, are more sensitive than others so it is really quite important to have tested your microphone beforehand. You then have a much better idea of how loud you need to speak. It is only on rare occasions that you will have the benefit of a sound engineer to control the volume for you.

If others speak before you take note of the volume they produce. Were they too close or too far from the microphone? Too much volume can distort the voice to the point of it being difficult to listen to. Too little volume can render the use of the microphone worthless and leave the audience unable to hear you.

The microphone is a friend Do not approach it with any sense of fear or trepidation, even if it is the first time you have used a microphone. Used properly it can be an absolute boon.

By amplifying your voice for you it will take away any strain that might be caused by trying to make your voice carry.

There are speakers who say they can manage without a microphone. They probably can for a few moments, but as their speech progresses they find it harder to keep throwing their voices. They lose the ability to produce those nuances of inflection that can add so much to the presentation.

Remember that if there is a microphone provided it is probably there because experience has shown that the acoustics are such that it is needed.

Treat the microphone as a friend, having accepted its presence you can afford to speak completely normally, safe in the knowledge that your audience can all sit back and hear you without having to strain to catch your words.

REMEMBER YOUR AUDIENCE

Having given thought to all other aspects of your delivery, remember that your speech is ultimately for the benefit of your audience.

You have hopefully, now made sure that they can sit and both hear and see you without any irritating distractions. Now you must make sure that they feel a part of your speech. Right through your preparation and now your delivery you will have concentrated on talking to them and not at or over them.

If you are being humorous, let them laugh and give them time to do so. If you 'kill' the laugh by following it too quickly with your next remark, they will tend not to laugh as your speech progresses for fear of missing the next sentence. You know your speech is worth listening to, so make it easy for them.

Try to relax as you speak and in doing so look at your audience. Establish eye contact with them around the room so that they feel that you are speaking to them individually as well as collectively.

Anyone who has ever taken part in amateur dramatics will have been told to speak over the heads of the audience to maintain the illusion of the part you are playing. In after dinner speaking the very opposite prevails.

YOUR PERSONALITY

I hope you will now begin to appreciate that there are many facets to making an after dinner speech. You have spent time and trouble preparing the wording of your speech and now you have to make sure that its presentation is worthy of that effort.

The final delivery, as you can now see, is equally important. In itself, it requires as much thought and preparation. The greatest need is honesty with yourself in rehearsing your delivery – there is no-one more conversant with your faults and foibles than you are. Try and remove those that might detract from your performance or irritate your audience but remember one thing: you have a personality all of your own which you want to project, so don't be too tough on yourself!

In many cases you will have been asked to speak, in the first place, because of your own personality. Don't kill it – let them have the real you! Be careful to consider the dangers I have outlined in preparation and presentation but don't be overawed by them.

7. Do's and don'ts of public speaking

DO GET THE FACTS

Are you sure you know where, when and what speech? Try and obtain this information in writing from the organizers. Otherwise write to them yourself setting out the details as you understand them. Someone will soon write back if you have got it wrong! Imagine spending hours of preparation on the wrong speech for the wrong occasion. Once you are certain of the basic requirements you can start preparation in earnest but not before.

DON'T TAKE CHANCES WITH THE ARRANGEMENTS

Having said that you should get the facts right and confirm them, not everyone does. I spoke on an occasion as part of a sixteen-week series of speakers to a very large society. All the speakers they engaged for the season were experienced and in many instances very well known. Even this did not prevent disaster. On one of their evenings, with only minutes to go before the speaker was due on stage, a very worried secretary rang the speaker to be told 'Is it this week – I thought it was next week'! Unforgiveable!

DO WRITE DOWN YOUR INITIAL THOUGHTS

If you are snatching odd moments of the day for your first stage of preparation, write down your thoughts. You may well find that with the other distractions of your working day you do not remember them again later when you need them. The more you jot down initially the greater the choice you have of material when it comes to a first draft.

DON'T TRUST YOUR MEMORY

I know that some of my own very best ideas and thoughts for speech content have been utterly wasted because I failed to commit them to paper. I now have one drawer in my desk that is full of scraps of paper with odd jottings of phrases, jokes, one liners and ideas and expressions. I often refer to it when asked to make a speech. It is not the tidiest of methods but it does ensure that I have a reasonable supply of material to jog my memory when it comes to the initial preparation.

DO ALLOW YOURSELF TIME TO PREPARE

As I have said, preparation is vital and there can be no short cuts, especially for those who are not used to public speaking. When you accept the invitation to speak, therefore, make sure you have set aside sufficient time to prepare properly. As you become more experienced you will find that the time you require becomes less and you may get to the stage when you no longer need to write out a speech in full at any stage of preparation.

I don't normally write my speeches out now. However, there was an occasion on which I was asked to give an address, by way of a tribute, at a very big memorial service. This was one time that a speech had to be written in its entirety. I set myself a very positive mental timetable for the preparation, culminating in a morning dedicated to writing a draft that could then be typed and edited to produce a finished article worthy of the occasion. Without that disciplined approach I know that I could not have prepared a satisfactory speech. Use the timetable approach and try to stick to it. Time soon runs out, even with plenty of advance warning. A last minute panic is hardly likely to produce your best work.

DO PREPARE YOURSELF

Nobody needs to feel better than you! Feel good, know you look good, and there is every chance you will be good.

Dress is an essential part of your own presentation. You don't need to buy new clothes to look well groomed, but you do need to check over what you intend to wear in good time, in case a visit to the laundry or the dry cleaners is necessary. Try the clothes on and take a cool clinical look in the mirror. Do you think you will look good when you stand up?

Are the clothes you have decided to wear appropriate for the evening? Consider co-ordinated colours where appropriate to create that pleasing look for your audience.

If your hair needs doing to make you feel happy and comfortable for the evening, make an appointment in plenty of time. If you're a man and need a good shave to look your best then plan your time to make sure you can fit one in before you go out.

DON'T DELIBERATELY LOOK A FREAK

This is a particularly dangerous way to try and make an extreme point to your audience. Deliberately dressing and appearing in a manner that is opposite to the majority of those present is discourteous to your hosts and as such is likely to antagonise your audience.

The best possible way to make any point, however extreme or controversial, is by the use of words. An outrageous personal presentation will only make a high percentage of your audience decide that they don't like you, even before you have opened your mouth. If you have paid them the courtesy of dressing and appearing in a manner considered acceptable for the function, they are much more likely to listen to you, however extreme the view you are trying to promote.

DON'T ARRIVE LATE

If you arrive at the last possible moment, or even worse, actually late, there is no way you can carry out the checks I have suggested, checks which are designed to make your presentation less stressful.

I always make it a golden rule to calculate the longest possible time from home or the office to a function and then add a further margin on top. There is no real problem in being early. You can usually find somewhere to sit quietly and collect your thoughts. You can give yourself all the time in the world to familiarize yourself with your surroundings. You will in other words feel comfortable and at ease.

By arriving at the last moment you will have failed to give yourself time to collect yourself on arrival. You will probably also have got into a state of anxiety as you rush to get there. You may also have worried your hosts unnecessarily into wondering if you are going to turn up.

DO CHECK ON ARRIVAL

Do make sure you know the complete geography of the room in which you are to speak. If you will be required to leave your seat to move to another point to speak, then make sure in advance you know where you are going. Have a really good look at the room and your own speaking position in it, as well as the position of your audience.

I once gave an after dinner speech to a small conference and they presented me with one of the worst possible lay-outs for a speaker – a hollow square. In this situation, those in front of you to whom you would normally focus the majority of your attention, are too far away to achieve a real empathy with them and those to the side are also too wide to be able to bring them into the company of their fellow audience. In these circumstances you are forced to change direction more frequently and more positively while you are speaking. If you have seen the room beforehand you have plenty of time to consider how you will handle the position of your listeners.

DO MAKE SURE YOUR NOTES ARE WELL PLACED

Place your notes where you can see and use them before you start. This will avoid a lot of fiddling with them once you are under way. If you need them don't be ashamed of them. Don't try and pretend you haven't got any, just place them naturally, that way you are less likely to drop them!

DO START SLOWLY

Always remember the golden rule to start gently and slowly. This will give you confidence and time to get into your stride. I mentioned earlier that one of the more common faults with inexperienced speakers is to start off at a breakneck pace to the consternation of their listeners. I cannot emphasize too often the need to take a deep breath and think what you are about to say rather than plunge into your speech inferring that the faster you go the quicker it will be over.

Give yourself and those who want to listen to you a chance.

DON'T DISTRACT YOUR AUDIENCE

This is especially important at the beginning of your speech.

I am continually surprised at the number of apparently normal and perfectly co-ordinated individuals who, the moment they rise to their feet become jerky and clumsy. I appreciate that nerves plays a large part in this problem but it is really the speed at which they rise that distorts their normal habits. If you try to do anything too quickly you are always in danger of becoming accident prone. I have seen speakers knock their chairs over in their haste to get to their feet! All this kind of action does is to totally distract the listener even before you have given him anything to listen to.

If you need to adjust the microphone because the height or distance from you is wrong, do it slowly and positively, the audience will wait – they are not going anywhere. I have seen speakers completely disconnect the microphone in their haste. The unfortunate result is that assistance is required to repair the damage to the utter confusion and distraction of the speaker before he has even started speaking.

DO USE THE MICROPHONE AS A FRIEND

You will have checked earlier how sensitive the microphone is and therefore how close you need to be to it or how much you need to throw your voice. Now stand up, speak up and ignore it. Try not to be conscious of its presence and speak as you would to a crowd of friends in your own living room. Remember it is not there as an enemy but merely to enable you to be heard throughout the room without having to shout or strain your voice and to enable all your audience to hear your every word.

DO STAND STILL

Stand comfortably, place your hands in a comfortable position and then remain as still as possible, without resembling a wooden dummy, so that your audience listens rather than watches.

DON'T FIDGET

Good microphones are of necessity extremely sensitive. This means that not only will they amplify your voice effectively but they will also make loud distracting noises if you fiddle with them while speaking. Do resist the common temptation of leaning on the stand as this can both cause unnecessary noises and, if you lean hard enough, vary the microphone's height.

I wrote earlier of people who play with the various items that are still on the table in front of them. I have in fact seen glasses of drink spilled over the speaker or whoever is unfortunate to be sitting next to him. I have seen crockery and cutlery knocked on to the floor with the inevitable crash. Even a man removing and replacing his spectacles fifteen times in ten minutes stays in my memory. In every case I don't remember a word they said and probably didn't at the time either!

DON'T SHUFFLE NOTES AND PAPERS

Having agreed you need to have your notes to hand for easy reference, don't let them become an extra source of distraction.

Put them where you want them and don't fiddle with them. When your audience is quiet and listening paper rustled can make rather a lot of noise, particularly if it's close to a sensitive microphone.

There was a time when I used to broadcast as an amateur with an overseas radio station. Before I was allowed to 'go live' any papers had to be spread out across the desk in front of me to avoid any sound of movement being picked up by the microphones.

The other danger with playing with your notes is the possibility of getting them out of order and even worse (if you haven't put that all-important string or treasury tag through them) you could drop them.

Never create problems for yourself by being careless with your notes. They are your lifeline – treat them as such.

DO TRY TO BE SINCERE

When talking to people the most transparent emotion is sincerity or the lack of it. If you do not believe in what you are saying you will find it hard to come across with any sincerity at all and your audience will spot it immediately. If you are patently sincere in what you are saying the listener will always give you his attention even if it does not include his agreement with your views.

DO TRY AND USE GOOD ENGLISH

The use of slang expressions jars on many people's ears and in some instances they may even find it difficult to understand your meaning. The use of well spoken English is a delight to listen to and will usually ensure the attention of the audience. Slovenly and lazy use of words on the other hand becomes trying to the ear of the listener. Be careful too about using jargon.

Another point to bear in mind is that there may be foreign visitors among the audience and it would be discourteous to exclude them by using obscure expressions.

DON'T UNDERESTIMATE THE INTELLIGENCE OF YOUR AUDIENCE

Being sincere and speaking good English are important but so is never underestimating the intelligence of those who are listening. Some speakers seem to feel the need to express themselves with patronizing simplicity in case the audience don't understand them. I recently attended a charity lunch where an eminent broadcaster was speaking. His script would have been more than suitable for a programme for five-year-old listeners. The audience was lost to him very quickly.

In fact he suffered the double indignity of an audience that was quietly talking amongst themselves whilst he was speaking and one that gave him a very loud but ironic reception when he had finished.

Give the audience the benefit of the doubt and assume they are as intelligent as you believe yourself to be.

DO USE YOUR NOTES IF YOU NEED THEM

I have advocated learning enough of your speech to give yourself a comfortable working knowledge. However, I do not believe the average speaker, particularly the beginner, can hope to memorize their entire speech. You will need your notes for two reasons in particular. It will be a great comfort to you just having them in front of you. Secondly, you will certainly need to refer to them as you progress.

You need your notes so don't be ashamed of them. There is no need to hide them from your audience. Put them quite openly where they will be easy to see and read. When you need to read them, do so. Never apologize for such references, treat the use of them as a perfectly natural action, which it is.

You will see very few speakers stand up without any notes whatsoever, however good or experienced they may be.

DO KEEP COOL

When you rise to speak do not ignore your environment and surroundings. There are many things that could happen during the course of your speech which you cannot prepare for in advance. Accidents can happen without warning and you need to keep a cool clear head in spite of your understandably nervous feelings.

Think while you are speaking and always try to keep an eye on what is happening around you.

I was at a dinner once where a wine waiter actually came up to the speaker in the middle of his speech, and tried to present him with his wine bill! The speaker quietly waved him away without letting it disturb his delivery. He retained his cool in face of circumstances he could never have anticipated.

Members of the audience can be taken ill at any time and are not always able to leave quietly. You might need to pause to allow help to be offered before continuing. Any such incident can be handled by a speaker who is in control of both himself and his situation.

DON'T PANIC

Having observed that unexpected incidents can happen which need to be dealt with coolly and calmly, obviously the reverse can apply.

There may be moments when sheer panic can set in so that a speaker is lost to both himself and his audience. However, if you are concentrating on the positive aspects of your situation it is much less likely. You have prepared a good speech thoroughly and well so have confidence in it and yourself. Just take a deep breath and give yourself a second or two to recover. The moment will pass!

DO REMEMBER TO LOOK AT YOUR AUDIENCE

I have tried to make it clear throughout this book that you are communicating with the listener.

Without your audience you haven't a speech. Do remember to look at them, they are on your side. They want to feel individually that your speech is for them and for them alone. Spread your glances around the room and avoid appearing to address one particular section of the room to the exclusion of the rest.

One of the reasons that after dinner speeches take place in fully-lit rooms is so that you can see your audience unlike a stage presentation where the audience is in the dark.

I was asked to make a speech recently in a theatre and I asked especially for the house lights to be left on throughout. This was to help the audience feel that they were a part of the speech and not watching a theatrical performance.

They want to share your speech with you, don't disappoint them.

DON'T GET OVER-CONFIDENT

Many speakers are terrified of their first speech but once they are into the swing of it they begin to enjoy themselves.

This is when over-confidence can creep in and cause a new set of problems. You have prepared a speech which you believe is within your capabilities to deliver and suddenly it all seems so easy. Why not try a few variations? Why not bring in a few of those rather ambitious ideas you had when preparing originally?

The reason 'why not' is that you are immediately running away out of control. You have departed from your prepared script and you will possibly even lose track of it altogether in due course. You will be deviating from your brief and you will not be sure where or when to stop. There is every likelihood that you will begin to ramble, losing the flow of your argument, or even repeating it. You alone will be causing your own downfall while believing how well you are doing.

Once you get started, if it does seem easier than you thought it would be, just be thankful and give the best of what you had prepared and resist temptation.

DO WATCH THE TIME

Having prepared a speech to last a given period of time in line with your original brief, watch the time as you speak. If there is a clock conveniently placed in the room this can help. If not, I suggest you remove your watch and place it in front of you before you stand to speak.

If you feel you are going to finish short of your planned time, don't worry, no-one will complain. Certainly don't try and pad out with material you have not prepared.

The real problem arises when you think you may over-run your time. Whatever you do don't attempt to speed up your delivery. You will not make the same impact on your audience if they sense you are rushing to catch up on time. It is far better to omit a point or two and proceed more directly to your conclusion.

There is a speaker I enjoy working with as toastmaster who asks me to tell him how long he has to speak immediately before he rises. He then starts his stop watch and always finishes on time – not really something recommended for the beginner.

DO REMEMBER YOUR FINALE

You have negotiated all the traps and pitfalls and you have almost finished your speech. Don't forget, though, that your ending is all-important.

Your audience have listened to your thoughts, your ideas, your humour and now you have to leave them. Remember you were going to finish with short and positive sentences. Don't be tempted to change your mind, especially if you feel it has gone well. If it's a toast you are proposing don't let it fall flat. Give it to them clearly and leave them in no doubt that you have actually proposed your toast.

Always bow out while you are in front, don't be tempted to extend a successful speech. I heard an excellent, humorous after dinner speech a while ago which received a well deserved and enthusiastic reception. The speaker, who was a professional and should have known better, was carried away by his applause and rose to give an extra few minutes. Unfortunately his actual speech was well prepared and when he reverted to an impromptu encore he virtually destroyed all the good that had gone before.

8. Conclusion

In writing a book that will, hopefully, help aspiring after dinner speakers, I have had to adopt a very general attitude to what I firmly believe is the 'art' of after dinner speaking.

I have been convinced for many years that after dinner speakers fall into three categories. First, there are those who are born speakers, able to stand with all the ease and assurance of a seasoned professional and entertain and, if needs be, educate an audience. Second, and by far the largest category, are those who with some help and assistance, together with the willingness to work at it, make very competent and acceptable speakers. Finally there are those who will, as a result of their own nervousness and even shyness never really enjoy making speeches.

In certain circumstances business or social pressures dictate that one has no option but to speak, but otherwise those in the third category are best advised to gracefully decline an invitation to speak. But for those who feel they would like to try and become proficient speakers I hope this book will be a help.

If one accepts that the normal occasions on which you are likely to be asked to speak are happy and sociable ones, then you too should enjoy yourselves. Don't face the event as if it were some form of sadistic punishment heaped upon you!

If you can project an air of calm enjoyment, even if the nerves are suggesting otherwise, then those forced to listen will believe that they too can enjoy themselves.

As one who has spoken on hundreds of occasions I can assure the reader that the nerves never go away, you merely learn to live with them and control them.

On the subject of nerves, there is no need to worry about being nervous and indeed it is a perfectly natural phenomenon. There is many a great actor who will tell you that without that tinge of nerves the performance itself is likely to suffer.

I know that some speakers have tried mild medication on occasions to calm their nerves but I would strongly condemn this practice, if for no other reason than the fact that it can detract from your speech rather than enhance it. I have already mentioned that alcohol before or during dinner will not calm the nerves but merely dull the senses that may be very necessary later.

If you are invited to speak, I would always suggest that you seriously consider accepting the challenge. When you accept it don't underestimate the task in hand. Give it serious thought and preparation and you will find that you will begin to look forward to the chance to deliver your speech to an audience.

The first time you speak there will always be the fear of the unknown but until you have stepped over the brink you will never know whether this might be opening up a new hobby, or even career, for you.

There is no particular type of person who makes a good speaker. They come from all walks of life and all strata of society. Many take it up almost by accident but once bitten by the bug want to keep trying, always striving to produce a better and more complete performance, always trying to master the ever changing occasions and audiences. I suppose I can claim to be one of those who fell into it by accident: the very first time I spoke I was told the only way I could possibly attend the dinner was by agreeing to respond for the guests! The now long defunct Caledonian Society of Aden has much to answer for!

The fascinating thing about making an after dinner speech is that regardless of what others may say, the one person who can really say how well you spoke – is YOU!

Index

THE WORK MATTERS SERIES